Anonymous

The Landing of the French Atlantic Cable at Duxbury, Mass.

Anonymous

The Landing of the French Atlantic Cable at Duxbury, Mass.

ISBN/EAN: 9783743413405

Manufactured in Europe, USA, Canada, Australia, Japa

Cover: Foto ©ninafisch / pixelio.de

Manufactured and distributed by brebook publishing software
(www.brebook.com)

Anonymous

The Landing of the French Atlantic Cable at Duxbury, Mass.

THE LANDING

OF THE

FRENCH ATLANTIC CABLE

AT

DUXBURY, MASS.,

JULY, 1869.

————•————

BOSTON:

ALFRED MUDGE & SON, PRINTERS, 34 SCHOOL STREET.

1869.

INTRODUCTORY.

A very general desire having been expressed that some account of the circumstances attending the landing of the French Atlantic Cable at Duxbury should be preserved in a form more compact and permanent than that of the public journals, the Committee of Arrangements of the Celebration to do honor to the occasion have caused the following detailed narrative to be made. It is compiled chiefly from the press reports, which were unusually full and accurate.

It is believed that the great event of the landing of the first Transatlantic Telegraphic Cable on American shores is important enough to possess, not only a peculiar local, but a general, historic interest, which merits a careful preservation of a record of all the circumstances connected with it.

THE COMPILERS.

THE TOWN OF DUXBURY.

It is not within the design of the compilers of this brief account of the "Cable Celebration" to give even a sketch of the history of Duxbury; and yet an allusion here to some of the circumstances connected with this ancient town may not, it is thought, be inappropriate.

The very name of Duxbury has a peculiar historic interest; for it connects us, in thought, with the first military hero of the early settlers of New England, the name of the seat of the Standish family in England being Duxbury Hall, and out of respect to that valiant hero, Myles Standish, who performed such distinguished service for the Plymouth Colony, and who settled in Duxbury about the year 1631, — six years before its incorporation as a town, — was it thus named. It shares with Plymouth the honor of being settled by several of those who came over in the "May Flower," and who signed, in her cabin, that immortal instrument whose spirit pervades American institutions to-day. No town could have had a nobler origin. In none repose the honored ashes of a more glorious ancestry; the inhabitants of none perpetuate names more truly illustrious, or more worthy of lasting reverence. Here dwelt the saintly Brewster, whose unswerving fidelity and serene faith were illustrated amid the severest trials. Here are still the remains of the homes of the heroic and dauntless Standish and of the wise and faithful Alden; and here Collier, and Howland, and Soule, the Southworths, the Bradfords, the Delanos and Spragues, played their worthy, and still un-forgotten, parts in the foundation of an Empire.

Selected as the abode of such men, in such eventful times, Duxbury has, as may be well supposed, an interesting, and, in some respects, a striking history, of which, now that recent events have called her once more into notice, she may well be proud. Formerly, in the way of enterprise, and daring and successful industry, the leading town of Plymouth County, though for a few years past, from the effect of unpropitious circumstances, somewhat tending to decline, it is believed that, under the new impulses which are now active, and with the new facilities for business and transportation, and the means of readier and easier access which are in contemplation, and which are sure to be established in the near future, she will once more take the high rank among her neighbors to which her noble antecedents give her a rightful claim.

The geographical position of Duxbury is all that could be desired, either as a place for business or for recreation. In the old days, her enterprise in maritime affairs made for her a world-wide fame, and Duxbury ships, built and owned by Duxbury men, and commanded by Duxbury captains, gave her an honored name wherever commerce unfurled its radiant flag. Along the shores of her beautiful bay, and by the borders of her quiet rivers, the scenes of cheerful labor told of that provident energy and thrift which bring prosperity alike to the employer and the employed.

As late as the year 1837, according to Winsor's history of Duxbury, there were built here nearly 12,000 tons of shipping, and the late Mr. Ezra Weston, for a long time considered the largest ship-owner in the United States, resided here. The names of the leading men of Duxbury, in these old days of her prosperity and renown, are now, for the most part, worthily perpetuated, not only by the present residents of Duxbury and Boston, but, in some instances, by those dwelling in the most distant cities of the globe, in the Westons and Winsors the Spragues and Drews, the Frazars and Lorings, the Bradfords and Aldens, who maintain well the fair repute of their progenitors.

The location of Duxbury, on the coast some thirty-five miles southeast of Boston, is exceedingly beautiful, and possesses many natural advantages which seem to indicate for it in the future a career worthy of its renown in the past, both as a place of business activity, and a resort for those who are seeking health and pleasure. It is situated on the shores of a bay some four miles long, by three wide, and which is protected by a magnificent beach some seven miles in length. Within this fine harbor is Clark's Island, a spot forever memorable, and consecrated by the first Sabbath worship on the shores of New England. Bancroft, in his History of the United States, thus graphically describes the experience of the Pilgrims at this place: "After some hours' sailing, a storm of snow and rain begins; the sea swells; the rudder breaks; the boat must now be steered with oars; the storm increases; night is at hand; to reach the harbor before dark, as much sail as possible is borne; the mast breaks into three pieces; the sails fall overboard; but the tide is favorable. The pilot, in dismay, would have run the boat on shore in a cove full of breakers. 'About with her,' exclaimed a sailor, 'or we are cast away.' They get her about immediately, and, passing over the surf, they enter a fair sound, and shelter themselves under the lee of a small rise of land. It is dark, and the rain beats furiously; yet the men are so cold, and wet, and weak, they slight the danger to be apprehended from the savages, and, after great difficulty, kindle a fire on shore.

"Morning, as it dawned, showed the place to be a small island within the entrance of a harbor. The day was required for rest and preparations. Time was precious; the season advancing; their companions were left in suspense. The next day was the 'Christian Sabbath.' Nothing marks the character of the Pilgrims more fully, than that they kept it sacredly, though every consideration demanded haste."

The beach of which we have spoken runs, in a general direction from north to south, from Cut River to the Gurnet, and towards its northern end it sweeps to the west, forming an extensive curve. In this curve, which is sheltered from the full violence of northeast gales, and directly opposite Rouse's Hummock, is the spot selected as the landing place of the French Atlantic Cable. From the Hummock to the old Bank Building, the terminus of the telegraphic cable, it is a distance of one and three-quarters miles. The cable is landed on the main land at Duxbury at the Old Cove, and is carried through Cove Street, a distance of one-eighth of a mile, to the Bank Building. From the Old Cove to the Gurnet by water it is a distance of seven and a half miles; by a straight course five miles. From the railroad station, in Kingston, to the Old Cove it is a distance of about five miles, a d from the latter to Standish's Hill three miles. Between these two points, running north and south, is the principal street of the place, called Washington Street. From the Old Cove to the Hummock it is a distance of one and a half miles, across a large tract of salt marsh, intersected by several small rivers. The telegraphic cable is landed on the beach at the point above described, carried in a trench across the ridge of the beach to the cable-house on the Hummock; thence, across the marsh, to the Old Cove, and from there to the old Bank Building.

It is impossible, as has been already hinted, to enter here into a minute description of Duxbury, or to give the details of its history, interesting as many of them are. No place has had more decidedly original and peculiar characters, and no place, perhaps, has more carefully preserved some of the sturdy virtues of the Pilgrims. In every great conflict since the settlement of the country it has borne an honorable, and, in some cases, a distinguished part. Thrilling stories of the daring of its inhabitants during the revolutionary war are yet told. Especially by sea, did its heroic men perform marvellous exploits, and illustrate

SECTION OF DUXBURY BEACH, on which the Cable is landed.

the courage of Massachusetts sailors. It gave to the first war
between the colonies and the mother country a larger proportion
of men than any town in the county, with perhaps one excep-
tion; and, as late as 1840, there were nineteen surviving heroes
of the revolution in Duxbury, whose aggregate age was 1,025
years, and the average over 78 years.* To the war for the
suppression of the late rebellion, also, it contributed its full share,
and kept the lineage of its honor unbroken. Like most other
towns whose inhabitants are chiefly engaged in maritime affairs,
Duxbury has its traditions of wonderful adventure, and hairbreadth escapes, as well as its fully authenticated records of
deeds of strange daring and splendid heroism; its tales of the
noble courage that has rescued the wrecked mariner whose ship
was stranded by the winter storm; of the skill that has defied
the tempest and navigated the globe, when to do so was a rare
achievement; its stories, too, of sadness, which cause the narra-
tor's voice to tremble when he tells them now; of the wanderer
who went forth and returned no more to the love that waited
sadly and longingly for the tidings that never came; of
mysterious losses; of ships that went down with all on
board;—all these might furnish the historian of Duxbury with
enough to make his narrative exciting, pathetic, and as interesting as the dreams of romance. Our business is only to leave
a record of the incidents of a great event of to-day, which has
lifted this quiet old town from obscurity to notice, and which,
we believe, may help bring back once more her ancient prosperity.

* Winsor's History of Duxbury.

2

THE FRENCH ATLANTIC CABLE.

WITH the history of the magnificent enterprise of organizing the French Atlantic Telegraphic Company, and its successful accomplishment of the laying of the cable, this little record has, of course, nothing to do. Duxbury considered itself fortunate in being selected as the point of landing, and desired to express its satisfaction thereat, and to extend its welcome to those who had accomplished the important work, in some worthy and appropriate manner. In anticipation, therefore, of the arrival of the steamers bringing the cable, a meeting of the citizens was held in Masonic Hall, on Friday evening, July 16th, at which the following resolutions were presented, and unanimously adopted :

Whereas, The Town of Duxbury has been selected as the landing-place of the French Atlantic Cable, which is expected to arrive within a few days; and *whereas*, that event will be one of unusual interest in the history of the town, as well as of national and world-wide importance, we, the citizens of Duxbury, deem it proper to show our appreciation of its magnitude, by celebrating it in some appropriate public manner, and, at the same time, extending the welcome and hospitalities of the town to those who shall have so successfully accomplished this important undertaking; therefore it is

Resolved, That a Committee of ten be appointed by this meeting with authority to make the necessary arrangements for the successful public celebration of this event. And it is further

Resolved, That we pledge to said Committee, acting on our behalf, our zealous coöperation, and that we look to them for a celebration on this occasion worthy the ancient renown of the old Pilgrim town of Duxbury.

In accordance with the above resolutions, a Committee was appointed, who immediately entered on the duties assigned them, and, as soon as possible, issued to many prominent gentlemen, including the Governor of the State, the Mayor of Boston, and

THE LANDING.

others eminent in the various walks of life, the following invitation :

FRENCH ATLANTIC CABLE.

The citizens of Duxbury propose to celebrate the arrival of the French Atlantic Cable on the shores of Massachusetts, and to extend their welcome to the officers commanding the expedition, by a public festival, to be held on the 27th instant.

They respectfully solicit the honor of your company on the occasion.

S. N. GIFFORD,	ALFRED DREW,
J. S. LORING,	WALTER THOMPSON,
ISAAC KEENE,	JAMES WILDE,
C. B. THOMAS,	JONATHAN FORD,
ALLEN PRIOR,	CALVIN PRATT,

Committee of Arrangements.

DUXBURY, July 20, 1869.

THE LANDING.

Meanwhile the cable fleet which left St. Pierre on the 18th of July, arrived off Duxbury on the morning of Friday, the 23d, and about two o'clock in the afternoon, the " Chiltern " with the cable, and her consort, the " Scanderia," came to anchor opposite Rouse's Hummock, about half a mile distant from the shore. The day was one of the most beautiful of summer, calm and bright; the surface of the ocean was unruffled, save by a light breeze, which only served to give an air of life and gladness to the waters, and everything in nature seemed to look propitiously upon the great work about to be completed. The moment the ships anchored they were surrounded by smaller craft of every description, and the scene became at once animated and picturesque.

Preparations were immediately made to land the shore end of the cable, but it was nearly half past four when everything was in readiness to proceed with the work. The huge rope, so to speak, — the shore end being about two inches in diameter, — had been pulled up from the tank in sufficient quantity to reach the cable-house on shore, and was coiled on deck. Two large sea-boats had been lowered from their davits, and brought up alongside, and side by side over them, after they had been lashed together, were spread a number of planks, and a capacious platform was thus soon erected, after the manner of a pontoon bridge. Upon this platform the cable was carefully lowered, and laid out in a very broad coil. Another large boat was attached, and fully manned by sailors. At a signal, the barge was cut loose, and the tars, bending to their oars, moved slowly and steadily to the beach.

Half an hour was thus occupied, and the crowd on shore, which had by this time become augmented to from five hundred to one thousand persons, watched the proceedings with the liveliest interest, ever and anon cheering on the sailors who were soon to end the glorious work. It was not many minutes from five o'clock when the boats grated on the beach, and the sailors, seizing the end, with a united pull, brought the terminus to dry Massachusetts soil.

Then a long, loud cheer rent the air, and continued along the shore as far as the crowd extended, and an artillery salute was fired from both the " Chiltern " and "Scanderia." There was a sudden and impetuous rush of the men for the landing point, while the ladies clapped their hands and waved their handkerchiefs. Many gentlemen seized hold of the cable, among whom were Collector Russell, of Boston, (who with others, had come down in the school-ship " Geo. M. Barnard,") and Stephen N. Gifford, of this place, Clerk of the Massachusetts Senate. An hundred hands grasped the cable, and with a jolly shout from the citizens, and many cheerful " Pull ahoys ! " from the sailors, the end was run up the beach over a ridge which limits the incursion of the tides, and over a short plateau, to the cable house, on Rouse's Hummock. The crowd followed, and were highly interested spectators of every inch of progress made. When the heavy work had been finished, and the assembly realized that at last the Empire of France and the Republic of America were united by a living, pulsating artery, another involuntary shout of gladness burst from every mouth.

CABLE HOUSE on Rouse's Hummock.

Messrs. Farley, Clark and Jenkin had made arrangements at the cable-house for testing the electrical condition of the cable, which was found to be perfect, and signals were at once sent and received to and from Brest, at the rate of five words per minute.

INCIDENTS.

Just before the cable was cut on board ship, the signals were strong and perfect, and several messages were sent and received. Among others one was sent to the Emperor Napoleon, announcing the successful termination of the enterprise; and Mr. Varley, the chief electrician, received one from his wife. One was also received announcing the rise of the price of cable shares in Paris.

As soon as the ships had anchored, they were boarded by a number of gentlemen from Duxbury, who were most kindly received, and hospitably entertained by the officers of the expedition.

It is proper to state here, also, that the City Government of Boston, believing that the important event should not pass unnoticed by the authorities of a city whose commercial interests will be so much and so favorably affected by the enterprise, appointed a committee consisting of Aldermen Benjamin James, John T. Bradlee and Moses Fairbanks, and Councilmen William G. Harris, James M. Keith, John O. Poor and George P. Denny, to make arrangements for proper demonstrations on the occasion of the landing of the cable. On the day succeeding the arrival of the steamers, Mayor Shurtleff, in company with the committee, visited Duxbury and tendered their coöperation, in the name of the city, in celebrating the event; which was subsequently done by the Mayor on the following Tuesday, and a salute of one hundred guns was fired on Boston Common by his command, and the national colors displayed from the public buildings.

THE CELEBRATION.

Tuesday, the 27th, was fixed on as the day of the celebration, and preparations for that occasion, as complete and extensive as the uncertainty attending the arrival of the cable, and the brief period intervening between that event and it would permit, were made. On the morning of that day, the sun was obscured by clouds and the weather threatened rain, but a gentle breeze from the southwest dispelled the vapors, and at noon the sky was cloudless, and the atmosphere delightful. The town was alive with excitement; flags were displayed in every direction, and many private residences were decorated. The residence of Mrs. William Ellison was adorned with exceeding taste, and attracted much attention. Over the door was a small and elegant triumphal arch formed of flags and streamers, and a second triumphal arch, formed of two lines of flags, was suspended from the trees in front of the lawn. Among these, the flags of America, France, and England were gracefully and lovingly intertwined,— a fitting symbol of the sentiments of peace and good-will which the electric cord, binding together the three nations, tends to fasten and cement.

Among the distinguished arrivals by the morning train were Sir James Anderson, Lord Cecil, Viscount Parker, Mayor Shurtleff, Mons. Birtsch, a distinguished French electrician; Judge Russell, Prof. Pierce, of Harvard College, Mr. Watson, the financial agent of the Cable Company, and many others. By the courtesy of Governor Claflin, two Parrott pieces of a section of the Second Massachusetts Light Battery were sent down, and, mounted on the summit of a hill near the scene of the festivities, at intervals belched forth their fire and smoke. The battery consisted of twenty-five men, under command of Lieut. C. W. Beal, and proved quite an accession to the appliances for the celebration.

A tent for the banquet had been erected on Abraham's Hill, an eminence overlooking the beach, the Hummock, the track of the cable across the marsh, the town, the bay, and a part of Plymouth. Here plates were laid for six hundred guests. The flags of America, France, and England, adorned the summit of the tent, and waved spiritedly in the breeze. By noon the scene from this point was full of interest and animation. In the first place, as has been intimated, nature herself favored the occasion with one of her gayest and most genial aspects. A summer's sun bathed the landscape in brilliant light; a refreshing southwest breeze woke the distant waters into life and motion, while an azure sky overspread the ocean, and doubled its own placid beauty by reflecting its deep tints in that mighty mirror. The blue waters contrasted delightfully with the green plain of marsh which spread out beneath, while a gay and joyous crowd added to the beauty of natural scenery the higher attractions of genial human converse and pleasant laughter. The fresh, pure breeze that came rustling from the bosom of the sea bore an exhilarating influence on its wings, which stimulated the health and appetites of all present. The crowd assembled numbered some four or five thousand people. The appearance of this crowd, as it thickly strewed the hill, or scattered into little groups under the shade of the trees, was exceedingly animated and picturesque. For the creature comforts of this multitude a number of caterers had erected several tents in which were dispensed the usual comestibles common to such occasions. Among the spectators was a large proportion of ladies, who redoubled the charm of the summer sunshine by the smiles and graces of their presence. A detachment of State constables, under the command of Major Jones, was in attendance to assist in preserving order. Their office, however, was a sinecure, good nature and civility being the order of the day.

THE BANQUET.

Shortly after two o'clock the distinguished guests arrived, and took the places assigned them at a raised table on the side of the tent. As they entered, the Plymouth Band, which for some time had entertained the vast throng with some excellent music, performed a spirited air, whose strains, mingling with the applause of the people, were expressive of a most enthusiastic welcome. The centre of the table was occupied by Hon. S. N. Gifford, the President of the day. On his right were Sir James Anderson, Hon. N. B. Shurtleff, Mayor of Boston, Hon. George B. Loring, Hon. E. S. Tobey, and others; and on his left, Lord Cecil, Hon. Thomas Russell, Collector of the Port of Boston, Hon. George O. Brastow, President of the Massachusetts Senate, Mr. Watson, and Mr. R. T. Brown, officers of the Company, Prof. Birtsch, a French electrician, Lieut. Vetch, of the Royal Engineers, Hon. James Ritchie, and others. Mr. Gifford called the assembly to order, and stated that, as they had assembled to celebrate the achievement of a great enterprise, it was fitting to invoke the blessing of Him under whose care and protection all things are achieved.

Rev. Josiah Moore, of Duxbury, offered prayer, after which nearly an hour was spent in partaking of the food with which the tables were laden.

At the close of the dinner, Mr. Gifford, before offering the first regular toast of the day, spoke as follows:

ADDRESS OF MR. GIFFORD.

Fellow Citizens: — We have assembled here to-day to congratulate each other on the accomplishment of a gigantic enterprise, and to say a word of welcome to those who have been mainly instrumental in initiating and carrying forward to a successful close this last great work of the age. We live in an age of wonders. Man seems to be master of the physical world. Apparently insuperable obstacles vanish at the touch of his magic skill.

A few weeks since, thirty days were required to reach the Pacific shores; to-day, the completion of that wonderful specimen of engineering ability, Yankee pluck and perseverance, the Pacific Railroad, places us in a week's time by the firesides of our friends at the Golden Gate. To-day we meet to rejoice over the landing of a line that not only annihilates the space between two continents, but, at the same time, if not a guarantee, is at least an earnest, that peace and good will shall forever continue between us and the mighty nations that occupy them. This is a great work, a great step in the advancing march of civilization, great for us, great for the world.

Let us then give to our friends from over the sea a hearty welcome, a welcome that will convince them that we are not only glad to see them, but that we appreciate the skill, the energy, and the persistent determination, that have originated, carried on, and completed this great enterprise.

At the conclusion of Mr. Gifford's remarks, Mr. C. B. Thomas, who acted as toast-master of the occasion, read the first regular toast:

" The President of the United States."

The band played " Hail Columbia," and Mr. Gifford called upon Hon. Thomas Russell, Collector of the Port of Boston, who responded to the toast substantially as follows:

REMARKS OF JUDGE RUSSELL.

It seems like a dream, that we are here in this quiet corner of our dear old colony, to rejoice over the laying of the cable which connects Rouse's Hummock with the habitable globe.

The generous applause with which you honor the President shows me that I am awake and at home. I am sure if this great man were here, he would join in your expressions of delight that this enterprise is happily completed; that such an addition has been made to the commercial facilities of the nation which he worthily represents; that this new bond of peace connects the old world with the new. I feel sure he will be glad to join with Congress in securing the rights of this enterprise by the impartial laws of justice, the best defence of commerce, the highest security of States, the true foundation of international law.

It came suddenly upon us; we feared, if I may say so in

3

Duxbury, that you meant to bring the cable in *clam et secreto*. It surprises us now, although it is not the first Atlantic telegraph; but it is a wonder still. The poet said of his lady:

"The blood within her veins so eloquently wrought,
That you might almost say her body thought."

And when we see these arteries of life — let me rather say these nerves of sensation — spreading over the earth and penetrating the sea, it seems to our fancy that the great globe itself has become a sentient being — instinct with thought, and thrilling with emotion.

Since Mary Chiltern landed on the rock, to the day when the Chiltern and her consort anchored on this coast, a vast series of years has passed — a vaster series of events. But we, children of the Old Colony, love to believe that all we celebrate to-day was there in the hearts of the Pilgrim Fathers, — the triumph of art and science, of which this is the crowning glory, the greater triumph yet to be.

The genius of Morse, the energy of the Fields — we will honor them whether they will or no — the skill and perseverance of Sir Samuel Canning and Sir James Anderson, whose knighthood of enterprise is a title to American respect; the guinea stamp of rank, the pure gold of manhood, such as her Gracious Majesty loves to impress with that stamp; the grand achievements of the great man in whose name you call on me to respond, and of the people whose leader he is, the great thoughts that are to thrill this pulse of the world — all were decreed when the free spirit of the old world sought its home in the new.

Do not wonder that I dwell on Pilgrim memories.

You can show us the dwelling of Alden; the Bible which he loved; the house of Standish, where he watched the little empire of which he was the guard, and looked forward, perhaps, to the greater empire which he helped to found; the well of which Brewster drank, running of that purer well of which all were to be free to drink, and here, as much as in Plymouth, we are on Pilgrim soil.

An undeveloped power lay hidden in the gray mass of wire coiled in the Great Eastern; soon the grave men of the Mayflower were engines to thrill the world.

One thought more, although it is a familiar thought. This is a victory of peace. The poet says:

> " Mountains interposed make enemies of nations;
> Lands intersected by a narrow frith abhor each other."

But our railroads level the mountains, telegraphs pierce the seas, and all nations and tongues and kindreds are made neighbors. The Emperor of France, sitting in his palace, can, by an electric spark, fire a battery on these shores.

But the echo which we shall send back will be " Peace and Friendship."

The three united flags of three great nations that waved in the waters of the bay last week, and which now adorn this pavilion, are a token of friendship, and may it last till all the powers of the earth shall be *united*-States.

The second regular toast was:

" The State of Massachusetts."

This was responded to with the " Star Spangled Banner," by the band, and Mr. Gifford then said:

I see present with us, to-day, a gentleman who has been a firm friend to this company from the start — a gentleman who for two successive years has had the honor to preside over the higher branch of the Massachusetts Legislature, being President of the Senate for the year 1868 and a part of the term for 1869 — a man who stood by the interests of this company when there seemed to be hardly a show of success, and when every member of the committee was opposed to the granting of a charter to extend a welcome and meet them in deep water, and who rejoices as much as any of us rejoiced when we finally succeeded in accomplishing the purpose we had in view. I have the honor to introduce to you the Honorable George O. Brastow, of Somerville.

Mr. Brastow was warmly received, and spoke as follows:

SPEECH OF HON. GEORGE O. BRASTOW.

Mr. President, and Ladies and Gentlemen : — I regret exceedingly that his Excellency, the Governor of the Commonwealth, is not present on this occasion, that your sentiment might be more appropriately responded to. Indeed, I should not have been here, friendly as I have been to this great enterprise which has now achieved such wonderful success, had I not expected that the governor, or some other member of the State government, would have been here to respond to your sentiment. But, sir, in his absence, I think I hazard nothing in assuming that the government of the Commonwealth of Massachusetts interposes no objection to the landing of the French Atlantic cable. [Applause.] Other than that, sir, I feel that the heart of the whole people of the Commonwealth beats in sympathy with your own people of Duxbury in welcoming the distinguished gentlemen who have been so foremost and so successful in this great enterprise. The legislature of Massachusetts, as you have said, at last rendered every aid that legislation could render, and granted the facilities that were asked for. The allusion made by Judge Russell to the old colony and primitive times reminded me of the landing, nearly two hundred and fifty years ago, from that little ocean-tossed barque of a company that received a much colder and more rigid welcome, and from another race, than that now bestowed upon our distinguished guests. That little barque, tempest-tossed for months, as it was, landing upon this barren shore, brought the seeds that have made New England what she is. The seeds of that civilization were brought from across the ocean. What we welcome to-day is one of the highest evidences, and one of the most brilliant results, of later civilization and later science. Mr. President, I regret exceedingly that the Governor is not here to speak for the whole people of the

Commonwealth, who, I can assure you, rejoice at the successful completion of the work which you to-day are celebrating.

At the close of Mr. Brastow's remarks, Mr. Gifford read the next regular toast, which was:

"*The Town of Duxbury:* Its inhabitants, the descendants of Pilgrim heroes, who planted on this very shore the seeds of our peculiar and noble American civilization — perpetuating the names of Carver, and Brewster, of Standish, and Bradford, and Winslow, and Alden, — attest their unbroken lineage by extending an enthusiastic and fraternal welcome to those who have achieved so magnificent an enterprise in the interest of the largest material prosperity, and on behalf of the unity of the human race."

The band immediately struck up "Yankee Doodle," and then the toast was responded to by Mr. C. B. Thomas, a native of Duxbury, as follows:

SPEECH OF MR. C. B. THOMAS.

Mr. President: I suppose there is no man with Duxbury blood in his veins who does not rejoice to behold this day, or who does not realize, in some degree, the magnitude of the event we are assembled to commemorate. Away from any of the great lines of travel and traffic, and — as the newspapers have taken special pains to inform the public during the past week, and as some of you have learned by rough experience, perhaps — somewhat difficult of access, this ancient town was sinking into obscurity, and some would have us believe into oblivion. But the French Atlantic Cable has found us out, and, in some sort, glorified us, and to-day there is not a place of its size on the American continent so famous. I have heard, sir, of but one instance of regret, one sigh of that conservatism which always dreads a change, one expression of reluctance that this bond of mystic power is to unite us to France. One man there is, I am told, so wedded to its old passive and waning life, that he doesn't "want them plaguey Frenchmen to get a foothold" on the sacred soil of Duxbury. For my own part, sir, I have very little fear of the French while the present Napoleon is the head of the nation. For, animated by an almost boundless ambition to perpetuate the glory of his name, he knows that the surest way to do so is to glorify France, and that her prosperity can only come from a peace which shall protect and foster her great industrial interests; and I am sure that he has little disposition to trouble his neighbors needlessly, especially one which is bound to him so closely as we are now.

We have assembled, then, without shadow on our spirits, to welcome and congratulate those who have so successfully achieved this great enterprise of uniting these two vast continents by so subtle and vital a tie. Mr. President, it is really one of the grandest events of the age, one whose importance, estimated by its possible and probable results, it is difficult to overrate. It is a splendid and marvellous triumph of energy, calling to its aid the might of imperial science. To think that time and space are thus annihilated by human skill, that within the hour which we spend together here, we may send a whisper across the wild Atlantic, defying the clamors of its elemental strife, and regardless of its gigantic protests, a whisper that might be a message dropped into the heart of a friend three thousand miles away, or a diplomatic message which, in an hour, might convulse the world, is a strange and startling thought. It is a fact, which, if it had been prophesied to those who first came to these shores, would have been thought as improbable and impossible as a journey to the moon. Nay, our whole American civilization — noble, potent, everywhere advancing and victorious as it is — would have seemed too magnificent a vision to be realized; a dream, tinged with purple light, and rich with regal harmonies, and yet only a dream; too improbable to be an inspiration. Their impulses and their hopes were not bottomed upon earthly things. And yet to their diviner inspiration and loftier motives, to their rugged self-denial, to their unselfish disregard of outward earthly attainment, are we this day indebted for all that America is, all that she has done for the world, and all that the world yet hopes from her; indebted, let us ever remember, for that supreme glory which has so lately crowned our nationality, at once with the winning splendor of the martyr's fidelity and the coronet of the victor.

Mr. President, it seems to me, that, apart from other and more important considerations which led to the selection of this spot for the landing of the transatlantic cable, there are some minor incidental facts which lend a touching sanction to the choice, investing it with a peculiar appropriateness.

And first of all is the simple but significant fact that we stand, to-day, as the descendants of the first settlers of New England, *upon genuine Pilgrim soil.* The feet of heroes, of martyrs, of saintly warriors, animated with the courage of the cross, which no danger could frighten or subdue, have pressed it. Their tears have watered it. On this very air have their prayers and songs of unfaltering praise, alike in the darkness of the winter storm and the sunlight of the summer harvest, ascended. This mighty ocean, which we have so conquered that only a second of time separates us from the old world, rolled as an almost impassable barrier between them and the friends they had left in the old homes. And, as we meet here now for this most worthy and fraternal purpose, we can well fancy their voices coming out of the lengthening shadows of the past to breathe a benediction over us. This is historic ground. There is Plymouth Rock, richer in elevating and kindling associations than the bloodiest battle ground upon the face of the globe. There is the home of Standish, the hero whose brave life the genius of poetry has taken for its theme and its inspiration. There is Clarke's Island, where the first New England Sabbath hymn went up on the wings of the tempest,

> " When the stars heard and the sea,
>   And the sounding aisles of the dim woods rang
>   With the anthem of the free."

And there, too, are the graves to which the weak and the faithful wearily sank, as to a welcome rest opening to a celestial glory such as none but a faith like theirs could picture.

And it is subdued and chastened by the spirit which appeals to us from these spots that we stand here to greet this last and mightiest achievement of the 19th century. Here, where the frail seed was sown; here, "where America began to be," we gather to pluck the ripened flower, and to wonder at the latest and grandest development of its life.

And then, too, to the son of a Duxbury woman, born hard by this very spot, is science indebted for the clearest revelation, and its most useful knowledge, of the strange and hidden depths of the ocean.

And from the very telegraphic plateau which this cable traverses did the beautiful contrivance of Lieutenant Brooke for deep-sea sounding bring the first specimens of the bottom of the ocean, from depths of more than two miles.

And, once more, it is fitting that this cable should land on a spot familiar to, and beloved by, and associated with, the man, who, next to Washington, has done more than any other to give permanent honor and dignity and renown to the name of America among the nations of Europe. For, putting aside all political and local prejudice, and looking only to regal intellectual power, and to a solid literature which is to remain as one of the chief pillars on which the dome of American fame and glory is to rest in the future, I think that Daniel Webster, take him through and through, must be regarded as *the Great American.*

And he loved, with a passionate ardor which became his great nature, this sublime old ocean. He loved this beautiful stretch of beach which borders it. The massive and solemn tone of the sea was sacred music to his ears; and it is a fortunate circumstance which selected a spot thus associated for this purpose.

Standing here, then, between "the grave of Webster and the harbor of the Pilgrims," in the name of the American people, we extend a welcome to those who have consummated this stupendous undertaking. The men who do these deeds are the champions of civilization, and we greet them with a cordial, earnest, enthusiastic "God speed."

When Mr. Thomas had concluded his address, the fourth regular toast was announced:

"His Imperial Majesty the Emperor of France."

In response to which "Partant pour la Syrie" was played by the band, and three cheers were given for the Emperor.

An enthusiastic gentleman, seated at one of the tables, called out at this point for three cheers for General Grant, which were heartily given.

The next regular toast,

"Her Majesty the Queen of Great Britain and Ireland,"

was then read. This was responded to with "God Save the Queen" by the band, and three cheers by the company.

"His Majesty Victor Emmanuel, King of Italy,"

was the next toast, and Mr. Day, of New York, was called upon to respond.

ADDRESS OF MR. DAY.

Ladies and Gentlemen : — I wish there were an Italian here to answer your kind toast, but as an American and a citizen of the United States, I will say that the two nations have the warmest regard for each other, and that there is not an Italian from the Alps to Naples who does not rejoice at the visit of an American to his shores, and who does not appreciate our sympathy and admiration. After some further remarks in this strain, the speaker said that he took pleasure in welcoming those of that nation who were present as his friends. It was well said that Duxbury was between the grave of Webster and Plymouth Rock. This speech, though quite brief, contained many excellent points and was warmly applauded.

The toast-master then gave:

"*The City of Boston:* among the first to welcome all measures which assure the highest civilization of the world, she will hail with joy the last of all the grand agencies to annihilate time and space, the two great obstacles in the progress of nations."

4

His Honor, Mayor Shurtleff, of Boston, was called upon, and on rising to respond apologized for detaining the company a few moments as he had just been informed that the telegraphic connection between Duxbury and Boston was completed, and waiting for a communication to be sent to the city. He said he had sent the following:

DUXBURY, MASS., 27 JULY, 1869, {
4 O'CLOCK, P. M. }

To the Citizens of Boston: Their Mayor representing them at Duxbury sends the joyful intelligence that pilgrim Duxbury is now united to their ancient city by a new bond of union, which may our Heavenly Father grant to be one for the good of us all.

Mayor Shurtleff then spoke as follows:

SPEECH OF MAYOR SHURTLEFF.

Mr. Chairman and Gentlemen: — For your courtesy to the city of Boston, which I have the honor to represent on this occasion, and for the very respectful manner in which the sentiment just expressed has been received, I thank you sincerely in behalf of its citizens and municipal authorities. Boston cannot be indifferent to the success of the great enterprise, the accomplishment of which you are here assembled to commemorate in a most honorable manner. We of the city rejoice with you in this memorable achievement. We hail it as another link that will bind us in harmony and friendship with the old world, and multiply our years of existence by the almost annihilation of time and space.

Let us join you, then, in most hearty congratulations for the results which will enure to you and to all of us in consequence of the happy completion of scientific and mechanical labors which, through the medium of your ancient town, will unite the interests and welfare of our new world to that which gave birth to our forefathers more than two and a half centuries ago. Let the relations of the old world and the new, now so close in thought and word, long continue; and may this union of continents and people advance civilization, and encourage all those good arts and acts which shall insure for the wide world a future of universal peace, and a repetition of millennial periods, everlasting in duration, over regions of unbounded space.

When I cast a thought, sir, upon what is now going on in this usually most quiet of all places, and behold all the merry-making and pleasantries of the day — vividly reminding me of the gala days of my own native city when personal liberty was compatible with good government — and when my mind reverts to bygone days, when, sir, my own forefathers were the guardians of this soil, I cannot but think of that gallant little band of pilgrims, who, leaving the land of their birth and heritage, sought, in the most inclement season of the year, under the severest hardships, a home upon this very shore — that here they might enjoy the greatest of all earthly privileges, liberty of conscience and the right to worship God according to their own belief and their own inward dictates. Can I forget, sir, can you forget, that we now tread upon ground which they have hallowed? Here, even beneath our very feet, are the identical sods upon which those venerated men once trod. Beside these hills and within these valleys once dwelt the patriarchs whose names are now our household words. Need I tell you that here once lived and honestly toiled that venerable man of God, the reverend Brewster? that on yonder hill, with the first Christianized aboriginal of New England, the valiant and undaunted Standish had his abode? that dotted around us, were once the habitations of those useful public servants, Collier and the Southworths, and that gallant (or perhaps I should say ungallant) Alden, the cooper-boy, who circumvented the redoubtable Captain and won the blushing Priscilla? You may yet feel happy in the remembrance that upon yonder green and ever pleasant island our Pilgrim forefathers — safely escaped from the raging billows —first, on the land of their hopes — on the land of liberty — worshipped, unmolested and untrammeled, the God of Israel, the God of their fathers, their own God; and there spent their first Christian Sabbath in Pilgrim New England, giving thanks for their merciful deliverance, and invoking the blessings of their Heavenly Father to strengthen their resolutions, sustain their principles, preserve them from pestilence and savage beasts, and to increase and multiply them as a Christian and law abiding people.

Could time permit, sir, I would ask you to pass with me over the placid waters that skirt your shores, and visit for a moment that once peaceful Saquish, now, indeed, threatening with the appurtenances of war, but once the friendly refuge in the half-starving days of the needy Pilgrims, that gave the first nourishment to our perishing fathers. We could visit with the eye, from your captain's mount, Old Plymouth, and its glorious remembrances, the Pilgrims' Spring, that assuaged the thirst of the first comers, the lofty mound where first aboriginal accents kindly welcomed the weary pilgrim; the sacred hill where sleep so many of the fathers, and hills and valleys innumerable, where once the fathers worked and prayed, and nurtured that spirit of freedom which has secured to Americans the glorious privileges we of the present day claim as our birthrights.

And now, Mr. Chairman, in closing my remarks, let me say that the important event which you are now commemorating should not pass off as an affair of to-day. Let the old spirit of indomitable perseverance that brought our fathers to this spot increase the exertions of your people. Let them rouse their latent energies and awaken to renewed vigor and useful thrift. Before the sounds of our retreating feet are heard upon your roads, let yours be loud upon your hearth-stones; and there resolve that Duxbury shall once again be the borough of the leaders; that here shall be wharves and warehouses, railways, and their concomitant enterprises and business. And then, happy may be considered the day that the great French cable, for transatlantic communication, was landed and securely fastened upon your shores. Then will prosperity, thrift, and happiness be, to abide with you.

Before taking his seat, Mayor Shurtleff said: When I came to Duxbury this morning, I had the pleasure of being taken by my most excellent friend, Sir James Anderson, to Rouse's Hummock. Here I found this message, received at Duxbury at forty-six minutes past nine o'clock, A. M., from the other side of the ocean:

St. Pierre, 27 July, 1869.

Sir William Thompson to His Excellency the Mayor of Boston:

I have the honor of transmitting to you the following telegram received this morning from Paris:

To His Excellency the Mayor of Boston, America:

The Prefect of Paris, rejoicing in this happy occasion of closer union between the two countries, begs that the Mayor of Boston will accept his best compliments and good wishes."

Deeming that my good friends of Boston would be unwilling that the occasion should pass without an answer, I immediately returned the following, which I am assured has been sent:

MESSAGE OF THE MAYOR.

DUXBURY, MASS., 27 JULY, 1869.

To His Excellency the Prefect of Paris:

The Mayor of Boston sends a most hearty greeting. May the new bond of union between the continents be one of peace, prosperity and amity, and may the cities of the Old and the New World rejoice in mutual congratulations on the great scientific accomplishment.

The next regular toast was then read:

"*The French Atlantic Telegraph Cable:* uniting two continents, may it be, to all time, only a medium of good will, and the promoter of an international peace as serene and undisturbed as that of the still ocean-deeps through which it holds its course."

Mr. Gifford introduced Sir James Anderson to respond to this toast, and he was received with warm applause, and heartily cheered.

When the applause had subsided he addressed the assembled company in the following language:

SPEECH OF SIR JAMES ANDERSON.

Mr. President and Ladies and Gentlemen :—I did not know
when I came into this tent whether I should be asked to speak
at all. I may, therefore, very probably, forget to say, or omit to
say, many things that I ought to say ; and I am afraid I may say,
perhaps, some things which I ought not to say. It is not often
that one meets so many natural orators at a meeting of any kind,
and I feel I am quite unequal to say anything so eloquent as I
have heard since I have been sitting here. But it has been my
lot to be connected with Atlantic cables since they have been
successfully laid, and in all the gatherings I have seen, I have
seen nothing like this. [Applause.] It would be a very cold heart,
and a very weak tongue, that did not feel inclined to say something with so much beauty, so much cordiality and welcome of
every kind, in such a scene, and with such unbounded congratulations as we have had here to-day. I would think very little
of myself if I could not say something, if not eloquent, at least
earnest and honest. [Applause.] I know very well that I must
appear at the present time to be standing and receiving all the
honors due to others. I have no claim personally whatever to
any honor for the executive part of the enterprise just completed.
I did not navigate the ship; I did not lay the cable. My part,
as superintendent in behalf of the shareholders of the French
company, was of a different kind, and required different duties.
I am extremely sorry that my colleagues, Captain Halpin, and
Sir Samuel Canning, and all those men of such great ability, are
not here to see and know, what I so often have told them, that
no country in the world could give them, or would give them,
such a welcome, as the country,—or State, if you like,—of Massachusetts.   [Applause.]

I do not envy the heart that does not feel some romance, and
a great deal of poetry, on the landing of a cable from Europe

so near the spot where the Pilgrim Fathers landed. When I first asked my friend, Professor Pierce, a year ago, where I should land this cable, and he told me Duxbury beach, near to Plymouth, I knew the history of the whole thing, and I had in my mind's eye the appearance of the "Mayflower" as well as any man in Massachusetts, or in Duxbury. [Applause.] I know well the honored names that have been mentioned here to-day, and I yield to no one in my respect for their greatness, and for their earnest energy, and God-fearing intellect, that brought them from a land crowded with political oppression to a land where they could act as they thought proper, and could overcome any and every difficulty that the God they loved and feared might put in their way. [Applause.]

I did not forget, and I felt to-day, when the reverend gentleman asked the blessing on this meeting, that the successful cable of 1866 left the shores of Ireland with a religious ceremony, very devoutly carried out, and that it would be very strange if New England had received this cable on her shores without a similar expression of heartfelt sincerity. God only knows whether electric cables will be a great implement in war, or be a great instrument in the cause of peace, but, at all events, they have become a great fact, and I would be forgetting and outraging all my sense of justice if I did not confess honestly here that the Atlantic Cable is indebted more to my friend Cyrus W. Field than to any other man living. [Applause.]

No man knows better than I do the intense energy of my friend, Mr. Field; although I have heard rumors since I landed on these shores that he has opposed this cable in many and divers ways. I would think it strange if he didn't. Mr. Field and his friends have embarked large sums of money in that enterprise, with all the energy natural to his character, and will defend the enterprise where he has placed his money. So far as honorable opposition goes, we should not regard it as anything but just, because we would do the same thing. [Laughter and applause.]   I have been told, also, since I came here, that there has been a certain amount of opposition to the landing of this cable.   It may be due to the same kind of enterprise; it may be due to Mr. Field and his colleagues, but I don't care for that.   I am quite sure that the American people will not be unjust; I am quite sure they will not allow any one to inaugurate an enterprise, and spend a million of money, to unite the two great continents together, without giving them at least fair play.   [Applause] I believe it would be weak and foolish, on our part, to ask for undue sympathy or partiality.   If we cannot work as well, or faster, we have no right to your support, and we will not get it, notwithstanding whatever sympathy you may have.

This cable is, therefore, laid on your shore as purely a commercial enterprise for weal or woe.   Every right thinking man and woman will trust it may be a great promoter and great sustainer of peace throughout the whole world, and of civilization and good feeling.   God forbid that it ever should be used as the fearful weapon of war which it may become.

Ladies and gentlemen, I have nothing to say for myself.   You were kind enough to give me three cheers; whatever that meant, I thank you for it.   I am an old hand at crossing the Atlantic Ocean.   I have crossed it more than one hundred times, and I have ever felt that I was, betwixt your nation and mine, something of an ambassador, seeking to carry good feeling and good fellowship, and I am proud to say I have as many friends in America, if not more, than I have in my own country.   [Applause.]   It is a matter of no small pride to me that, after having for twenty-eight years been always upon the ocean, I have at last drifted into this singular enterprise of laying cables under the ocean, until we can now, or by this time next year, we will, in all human probability, be able to communicate, in a few hours, and in an ordinary commerce in a few minutes, all the way from California to Calcutta.   These are great times; the rising generations must work up to them, and doubtless will.   I am quite unequal to say what I would like to say, and in the manner I would like to say it. I would like to express to you how proud and pleased I am at this demonstration — a thousand times surpassing anything I expected to see. I did not even know, until I saw in the papers, that this celebration was to take place, and by some chance I was not invited. I did not hesitate to come, however, yet not for the sake of making a speech; but I hold I would a be poltroon if I could see all this got up in honor of an enterprise in which I had a small share at least, and not be warmed up to tell you that I truly, cordially, and earnestly thank you. [Applause.] One word more, gentlemen, and I am done. I would like to remind you again that I am returning thanks for gentlemen who had the real responsible charge of the expedition, and the operation of laying the cable, the labor of which was more than you have any idea of. Mentally weary, they have gone away to Niagara and other places to refresh themselves during the week before they leave for home. That they are not here to thank you, I am very sorry, because they would then know something I know of Americans, — of the great hospitality and unbounded generosity which I have always met. I am sure they would be very glad to thank you earnestly as I do. In their name, and in my own, I give you hearty thanks. [Applause.]

The next toast proposed was:

" *The Boston Board of Trade:* the representative of Commerce, in all ages the pioneer of a richer civilization, it has, in the electric telegraph, its most potent and cunning ally."

SPEECH OF HON. EDWARD S. TOBEY.

Mr. President, Ladies and Gentlemen : — I regret, not less on my own account than on yours, that the distinguished President of the " Boston Board of Trade " is not here to respond to the appropriate sentiment by which the name of that institution has

5

been connected with the interesting event which has brought us together.

If I were to take counsel of my judgment only, my remarks would be very brief; but the presence of so many faces familiar to me in youth, prompts me rather to follow the impulses of my heart in performing the duty which has been assigned to me by your kind invitation. The memory of the honored dead who were natives of this town, with whom in the past it was my privilege to be associated,—the fact that here in my youth some of my happiest and most permanent associations have been formed,—conspire to deepen my emotions on this auspicious occasion, and to place me in most cordial sympathy with the feelings which animate you in celebrating the event of to-day.

The traditional history of this ancient town shows that it was once foremost, not only in the foreign commerce of the Commonwealth, but of the United States. To speak of the character of the numerous first-class ships which have been built here, would be to recall the names of the best mechanics and skilled artisans of the whole country.

To speak of the men who commanded those ships, would be to make honorable mention of intelligent and eminent navigators, who, with the flag of the Republic at the mast-head, guided their ships into nearly every commercial port of the habitable globe. The landing of this telegraphic cable is of no mere local importance; and while it must give a historic prominence to Duxbury, and, we may hope, also a new impulse to her varied interests, it is to be regarded chiefly as an international enterprise, and as a new bond of sympathy and of common interest between our early ally and the United States. In carrying forward this great work, American and foreign capital and enterprise have been united, so that it literally belongs not to one nation alone. Would that a similar spirit of enterprise and employment of capital on the part of the citizens of the United States, under the fostering policy of the government, would now restore the ocean commerce of the country under the American flag to its once prosperous condition.

The representatives of foreign nations now present, will, I am sure, pardon my American feeling when I state that the American flag does not wave over a solitary *steamship* which crosses the Atlantic.

This fact, humiliating as it is and ought to be to our national pride, is one to which I desire to call the attention of the whole country. Of more than seventy steamships which now ply between New York and Europe, not one is the product of American skill and industry. If I am asked to account for this extraordinary fact, let me say that it is mainly to be attributed to the unfortunate and unwise policy of the government of the United States, and not to a want of enterprise on the part of her citizens. The time has been when the flag of this country was carried by her "merchant ships," in successful competition with those of every commercial nation. The war for the maintenance of the Union and the life of the government, appealing to every energy of the people, has so entirely absorbed the public mind and the persons who represented it in Congress, that the great shipping and navigating interests of the country have been sadly neglected — an interest, whose importance in a national point of view, can scarcely be estimated.

England has sagaciously taken possession of a large part of the trade on the North Atlantic by her efficient and successful steamships. France has shrewdly followed her example by granting mail subsidies on a scale of liberality equalled only by her great naval and commercial rival. Why should not the Government of the United States, at once adopt the same stimulating policy, by the remission of duties, and taxes on cost of construction, and by mail subsidies, and thereby bring into existence a fleet of steamships for ocean service worthy of her skilful mechanics, her enterprising merchants and seamen, and regain her once proud position as a first-class naval and commercial power?

It has often been assumed that the people of the West are wholly indifferent to the existence and development of ocean commerce under the American flag by the influence of liberal legislation. In my intercourse with them, whether in Commercial Conventions, Boards of Trade, or in Washington, I have ever found them friendly to the measures necessary to restore the flag of their country to its proper relative place on the ocean, and why should they not favor this great *national* interest when their own local interests have been so largely and rapidly promoted by enormous land grants and pecuniary aid which have brought into existence a trans-continental railway, while its projected branches and rivals will doubtless yet draw to them the further liberal aid of government?

Does it become America to pay to foreign nations annually from twenty to thirty millions of dollars in gold for the transportation of merchandise and passengers which might and ought to be carried in her own steamships? Would it not be wiser to pay at least a part of the money expended for ocean postal service for the transportation of mails by steamers to be *constructed, owned and navigated by her own citizens?* At the beginning of the late war there were only three vessels of the American navy at hand to defend our harbors and coasts. The merchantmen were then called on to blockade a coast of two thousand miles and to reinforce her navy at different periods during the war by tens of thousands of seamen drawn from the merchant service. Thus evidently dependent on the mercantile marine in emergencies, how can the United States maintain her position as a first-class maritime and naval power without pursuing as liberal a policy towards her shipping interests as England and France have respectively adopted towards theirs? The influence of the electric telegraph and of steam is rapidly bringing the people of all nations into more intimate relations. A combination of circumstances is conspiring to cause an ever increasing and vast immigration to our shores, and to develop the varied

"OLD COVE." The point where the Cable was brought to the main land.

and almost inexhaustible resources of our country. This must be regarded as one of the most potent agencies in promoting the commerce of the world and of advancing Christian civilization.

Let us therefore welcome the people of all nations here, encouraged by the fact that, in leaving their native land, they leave also the flag of their nation, content, and even desirous, to accept American citizenship, under a pledge of loyalty to the ensign of the Republic, that truest symbol of human rights and of popular sovereignty, transcended only by that still more sublime emblem, the banner of the cross, on whose ample folds shall ever be inscribed the soul-inspiring sentiment, " By this we conquer."

Mr. Thomas then read the following toast, which had been handed to him by a lady eighty-six years of age, the widow of the late Deacon George Loring, one of the most respected citizens of Duxbury. It was in Mrs. Loring's own hand-writing, and, as a specimen of penmanship, might, Mr. Thomas said, rival the chirography of most young ladies of eighteen :

"In memory of the past generation of ship-masters and ship-builders : May the electric spark now kindled so animate the coming generation that it may worthily fill the places of the past, is the wish of an 'Old settler.'"

Mr. Gifford called upon Dr. George B. Loring to respond.

SPEECH OF HON. GEORGE B. LORING.

Mr. President, and Ladies and Gentlemen : — When the mariner has been tossed for many days on an unknown sea and in thick weather, he avails himself of the first lull in the storm, the break in the cloud, and turns to the first glance of the sun, that he may take a new observation, and ascertain, if possible, where on the earth's surface himself and his ship may be. I call for the reading of the resolution — "The memory of the past generation of ship-masters and ship-builders of old Duxbury." We are at last, thank God, at home once more. We tread the dear old native soil. We are called to the association of those whom we have known and loved, and seen face to face. I have followed the distinguished gentlemen who have preceded me — have been carried back to the days of the Pilgrims — have listened to the policies of States; have heard how, a half century before Christ, submarine labors were performed beneath the waters of the old Italian rivers; have been borne to the ends of the world on the wings of commerce — and now I come back with you to this spot, with all its memories and charming associations.

I congratulate myself that I have been allowed to respond to the toast offered by the venerable lady of this town, with whom my relations are so intimate, and whose virtues adorn the home which some of us have loved so well. " The old ship-masters and ship-builders of Duxbury!" What memories do their names awaken! Their lives form a part of that history of this town, which makes it a remarkable illustration of the advancement and progress for which this age is distinguished. They gave Duxbury a name in all the great markets of the world, and made it a familiar household word in Antwerp, and Hamburg, and Liverpool, and London, long ago, in the vigorous periods of commerce, and when the names of the Giffords and Thomases, who clothe it with modern renown, were yet unknown. Forty years ago, sir, I was led along that beach, now so famous, a mere child, listening to the words of these very men, who are now gone. I shall never forget them. From that day to this has gone with me the memory of George Loring, the firm and honest and reliable Puritan, bearing in his veins the blood of John Alden, and presenting in his daily life an example of integrity and wisdom which we all might follow — the companion through life of her who offered this sentiment — and the fast fraternal friend of him who led me through the early days of childhood and youth. I ought not to forget the name of George Loring while I live. And who need be reminded here of the Sampsons, that stalwart race whose axes swung the brightest and sharpest, and whose hammers, as they drove the treenails, wakened me at dawn, even in the long summer days. Can we ever forget the name of Frazer, whose virtues have fallen upon at least one of those worthy sons of Duxbury now before me? And the Smiths, and Drews, and Soules, and Westons — a long list of enterprising and honorable men, who gave this town its wealth and distinction in early days, and whose service has now fallen upon many now before me — many who perpetuate their names and inherit their good qualities — shall not all these be remembered while Duxbury — Duxbury of old, and the new and regenerated Duxbury, shall stand?

The old ships may be gone; the "Cherokee," the "Choctaw," the "Susan Drew," models in their day of the best naval architecture, may have perished; but the good name of their builders and masters still remains, and will remain so long as the commercial world shall set high value on solid ships and honest merchants. These were the men who walked with me on the beach, and these are their ships. The manners and customs of the olden time were theirs still. The venerable form of John Allyn, the old divine, stern and incorruptible, with his silk stockings and small clothes and shoe buckles, stands there in the group, with his hands pressed upon my head, asking, in tones of thunder, "What are you going to do with this boy?" — while the sands of the beach seemed opening beneath my feet, and the awful weight of an old theological verdict seemed to crush me to the earth. But now comes the modern picture. "May the electric spark now kindled so animate the coming generation that it may worthily fill the places of the past." That energy which once gave Duxbury its renown, and which has slumbered so long, has now a newly opening field of labor. All the modern achievements in art, and science and literature and life are now before them. Their little quiet town has sprung by sudden impulse into new life. Through it now throbs one of the arteries of a busy and toiling, and vigorous and progressive world. It is the portal through which, in an instant, the thought of the great empire is transmitted. May it be a portal of peace. There now appear before us the three great powers of the world — France, England, and the United States — bound together in a common service, and one of the bonds is here. This triple alliance may accomplish much if made for a common purpose — the growth and advancement of the highest civilization. Dissimilar in many characteristics, they may learn of each other how to live. The lesson of free government in all its vitality, the United States are daily teaching.

From France we may learn how an industrious people may cultivate all the arts of life, develop the finest tastes, avoid the dangerous extravagances of modern days, and study the practical economies which add so much to the domestic comforts, and to public prosperity. To England we may turn, in these later days, for our lesson in the genius of progressive statemanship, and learn from the philosophy of Stuart Mill what manhood suf-frage really means, from John Bright the sagacity of a large-minded publicist, and from Gladstone how the policy of a great empire should accommodate itself to the popular wants and demands. In the great civilizing work, let these nations stand together, the great tripod on which advancing civilization may rest. That our companions in this association will respect our endeavors to preserve the perpetuity and strength of our government hereafter, I cannot for a moment doubt. Let us have, then, an honorable peace, founded on mutual respect for each other, and a determination to be guided by strict justice in all our intercourse; and as time goes on, when the three Pacific Railroads predicted by Mr. Seward shall be completed, and my friend, Sir James Anderson, shall have laid all his ocean telegraph cables, Sir James will pardon me, if I predict that New York will become the centre of the exchange of the world, and London will be tributary to New York. This is not too much

to anticipate. It is not too much to promise the " coming generation " of Duxbury boys, who are to make good the memories
of their sires.

Mr. Gifford then said that a motion had been made that, when
the meeting adjourned, it be to meet at the call of the first
whistle of the first locomotive that came into Duxbury, and he
called upon the Hon. James Ritchie to speak to that motion,
which he did in a very happy manner, expressing the hope that
the time was not far distant when that whistle would be heard.

The next toast was:

" The Ladies,"

which was briefly responded to by Lord Sackville Cecil.

RESPONSE OF LORD CECIL.

Mr. President, and Ladies and Gentlemen : — You have heard
the request made to me to respond to this toast. I am sure you
will join with me in thanking the ladies who have provided for the
company, for their kindness, and for honoring this occasion with
their presence. I am a young man, inexperienced, and not used
to speaking, and I may not say more. I trust that this may be
a sufficient excuse. Allow me, in sitting down, to express the
respect I feel for the ladies. [Loud applause.]

The next toast was:

" *Science :* with imperial thought and invincible power it subdues the
wildest and most fearful elements of nature, and binds them to the service
of humanity.

Hon. Charles Levi Woodbury was called upon to respond.
He said :

REMARKS OF HON. C. LEVI WOODBURY.

When I stood upon the shore on Friday afternoon and saw
the systematic, quiet and business way in which the cable was
landed from the steamers, and connected at the house with its

6

appropriate motors and instruments, I was impressed that this latest wonder of the world had already passed from the thaumaturgic class into the practical and ordinary business of life. It was my fortune to see, at Washington in 1837-8, at the capitol, Professor Morse make the first public exhibition of his telegraph. I recall it as though it were yesterday. Two reels of insulated wire, resembling bonnet wire, and each said to contain three miles in length, an old clumsy trough battery, where the acid was turned on and off every few minutes, — his leaden type cast for the forms which his signals have always had, a port rule of two feet in length in which to set them up, his recording apparatus and a folio copy of Webster's dictionary, with every word numbered in red ink. I think I can see it all before me now. There was no business electric telegraph in the world then. It was not till 1844 that Morse's own was practically set up. Suggestions, glimmerings, of an electric telegraph and partial experiments had preceded this epoch, but the thought needed a devotee whose inspiration should serve as a constant battery to his energy, and for this it had waited almost a century, growing slowly, but not ready for a practical career.

Let me briefly go back into the history of one hundred and twenty years ago, or thereabouts. A man who had the fortune to be a Boston boy and an Englishman — one Benjamin Franklin — was experimenting to ascertain whether lightning and frictional electricity were identical. He had already invented his conducting lightning rods of metal, and he now attached to the rod on his own house some bells to be operated by a galvanometer, whenever the fluid should pass down the rod, giving directions to his family that if the bells should ring in his absence, they should take some Leyden jars, and charge them at the rod, for his inspection on his return.

In time, a cloud passed over, the bells did ring; their call was obeyed, the jars charged, and the identity of the two fluids soon established. This was the first telegraph communicating intelligence by pre-arranged signal through the motive force of electricity. It was, in fact, a sound telegraph.

A few years after, he insulated a wire on the draw-rope at the ferry, on the Schuylkill, and sent his electric spark across the river, using the water, as he thought, as the conductor, and the wire completing the circuit; with this he set fire to spirits of wine across the river.

Here are the germs of this great practical, world-wide system of telegraphing we are now celebrating; and yet Dr. Franklin, although actually making and using an electric telegraph, never conceived the idea of applying the thought to the business purposes of the world.

In France, in 1787, the traveller, Arthur Young, saw in use at the Hotel des Invalides, the first known electric telegraph for actual correspondence between individuals, but still as a mere ingenious toy.

It is not disparagement to omit mention of the names of the ingenious men here and in Europe who have added by valuable suggestions and experiments to the progress of that now well defined thought, a business electric telegraph, one of whom I see before me (Dr. Jackson). The mechanism for handling, and the laws of the motor, were themselves to be ascertained before the application could become practical. Galvani and Volta found the best motor: so much for Italy. Denmark through Oersted, gave electro-magnetism; France, through Ampere and Arago, gave the electro-magnet; England, through Daniel and Grove, found the constant battery without which galvanic telegraphing would have remained a toy until to-day. America gave the insulation and suspension on poles for land telegraphs through Dyar, and had explored, through Professor Henry, the mechanical power electro-magnetism could exercise at great distances through a single connecting wire.

Thus were the materials for a practical telegraph collected, and out of these, able men of Europe and America soon organized telegraphic systems, and set them at work. America adopting Morse's system, and England that of Wheatstone.

Cable telegraphs followed the land telegraph, and, if my information is right, England has the glory of leading in the practical cable experiments, the first one laid across the Channel being still in use, as good as new — and to her electricians and engineers the development and perfection of the cable lines eminently belong, while thus far other countries have only aspired to share in the financial aspect of these enterprises; and this reminds me that I should say as a patriot to Sir James Anderson, that though these three times that he has brought a cable to our shores, we have said "Welcome, Englishman," yet that this thing is growing personal, and if he lands another here before we send one to his continent, we ought to deem it a national reproach.

I have referred to these matters of history because they include the great thought which underlies modern civilization, and exemplify the usefulness developed by following out new observations with careful experiment and reflection. In mechanics we follow and endeavor to imitate and utilize in our machines the curious mechanical arrangements and processes that we observe in use in nature: the triumphs of civilization in this line are mainly imitative developments of the great architect's work. The electric telegraph is not of this sort. There is nothing like it on the planet, nothing in nature to suggest its idea. It is a creation of the intellect alone, evolved as a germ one hundred and twenty years ago, developed, by the combined inventions and observations of a hundred inquiring men of science, into a grand nervous system of instantaneous sympathetic communication, already connecting four continents and many islands together like Siamese twins, so that within a few seconds states, nations, and the people of continents may thrill together under the influence of an idea and the impulse of one thought, conveyed to each other more swiftly than the air can carry the sound of a horn, or the brain can communicate its will to the hand, and guided to the objects of its impulse by a law as resolute as that which guides the planets in their course.

The force, created by God for the purposes of a final civilization, had lain, since the creation, waiting for the brain of utilizing science to reach the appreciative level, and, in a single century afterwards, this practical instrument of the world's progress and civilization stands matured, in wide-spread usefulness on every continent and in almost every ocean, a monument of the power of combined thought.

We recall what seems to us the spontaneous seed and growth of this idea, whose fruition is before us, and I ask is there not in the mysteries a law of God touching the generation, growth and expansion of ideas in the human intellect, to us unknown, but fixed, broad and certain as the laws governing material nature? And while we claim for men of science that keen appreciation of the laws of observation and logic, whose application requires in some sort, of the working priesthood of modern civilization and progress, a vestal abnegation to patient study, close attention and clear logic, as means of invincible power over the hidden secrets, may we not reasonably believe that there are other germ ideas now open before us, whose growing development, under their labors, will give humanity, in the future, a higher lot, a wider knowledge, a purer happiness, and a kinder brotherhood on earth than we have yet dreamed of.

Mr. George Frazer, a former resident of Duxbury, offered the following toast:

" The seeds of the " Mayflower," though planted in New England's cold December, have germinated, taken root and flourished, until their fruits are known the world over."

The president then announced the first message over the land telegraphic line from Boston to Duxbury, as follows:

"The Franklin Telegraph Company sends greeting to the Cable Telegraph Company, and hopes that the marriage which has just been completed between France and the United States will be a happy and a fruitful one, and that neither party will ever sue for a divorce." [Laughter and applause.]

Sir James Anderson said he had omitted, in speaking, to give due honor to those scientific men of America who had given their attention to the science of telegraphy. He should fail in his duty if he did not supply the omission, and say how much they were indebted to Professor Morse. No name in the science of telegraphy could ever be greater than his. He also wished to thank those gentlemen in Duxbury who had assisted the cable officials. He then went on to compliment Mr. Gaines, the chief clerk, in whom he thought the company had made an excellent selection.

In reply to the gentlemen who had spoken of the American flag disappearing from the Atlantic, he did not doubt but that the solution of that was as clear as the sun at noonday. He maintained that with free trade and fair play the American flag could, and must, resume her share of the carrying trade between America and England.

At this point the exercises were broken in upon by an incident which created the wildest enthusiasm.

At six o'clock in the morning, fifty stalwart laborers, under the superintendence of Mr. Gaines, the clerk in charge, had busily set about the task of conveying the cable from Rouse's Hummock into the banqueting tent, where, it was hoped, it would be fixed in time to send messages, during the dinner, to and from Brest. The work of conveying the cable along the marsh proved a heavier task, however, than was anticipated. The sun was broiling hot, the long coils of cable were very unwieldly and of great weight, and the difficulty of getting it across the different creeks was so formidable, under the circumstances, that the men, anxious to take part in the festivities of the day, refused once or twice to proceed. By the good generalship of their superintendent, however, they stuck bravely to their task, and by six o'clock they triumphantly hauled the cable into the tent, amid the cheers and congratulations of all present, and a deafening salute of artillery. The rope with which it was hauled was enthusiastically seized by many volunteers who pulled lustily; and those who did not move on were either shouldered aside or had their toes trodden on, as gentle hints that they must get out of the way. During these interesting proceedings, the guests crowded round the cable, and stood upon the tables to catch a sight of what was going on, while the band played an inspiriting air, amid which the great company dispersed.

CLOSING FESTIVITIES OF THE DAY.

The festivities of the day were appropriately closed by an elegant entertainment given by George W. Wright, Esq., at his splendid residence. Among those present were Sir James Anderson, Governor Claflin, Lord Cecil, Viscount Parker, Hon. N. B. Shurtleff, Mayor of Boston, Messrs. Watson, Brown, and Gaines, of the Telegraph Company, Hon's. Charles L. Woodbury, George O. Brastow, and other distinguished guests. The evening was enlivened with music by the Germania Band, of Boston, dancing, and speeches by Sir James Anderson, Governor Claflin, Mayor Shurtleff, Viscount Parker, and Hon. C. L. Woodbury.

Sir James Anderson, in proposing the health of the host and hostess, said:

He regarded this as something more than a convivial feast, elegant and perfect as it was; a model he would say, even for English homes, and he doubted not his French friends would say worthy of Parisian emulation. But it had a higher purpose, a sacred meaning. It warmed heart to heart, and only needed to be generally extended to knit nation to nation. Coming to himself and friends as strangers, holding accidental position, he received it as a pledge of a long and warm friendship, and would treasure it as brightest among the jewels of memory. He would make it the inspiration of higher purposes, and more active earnestness to cause his countrymen to appreciate the value of American friendship and the refinement of American hospitality. He would tell them, without reserve, that England's proudest glory, its virtuous home and free hospitality, had successful rivalship here in a quiet country town.

He was followed by Governor Claflin in a similar strain of happy congratulations, and by Mayor Shurtleff, who spoke in a genial and happy manner. Lords Parker and Sackville Cecil responded to calls for speeches, paying many compliments to the coterie of beauty around them. Hon. Charles Levi Woodbury closed this part of the entertainment with a speech full of sparkling humor, which called forth the laughter and applause of all present.

At a late hour, the guests separated with a pleasant and abiding conviction of Duxbury hospitality, as illustrated by Mr. Wright, and heartily gratified with the events of the day.

APPENDIX.

As it is thought that some account of the origin, laying, and method of working of the French Atlantic Cable may be interesting in this connection, the following extracts, the first from the *Boston Herald* of July 24th, and the second from the *Boston Daily Advertiser* of August 31, 1869, are given. The *Herald* says:

The concession for the building, laying and working of the present cable was granted to Baron Emile d' Erlanger of Paris, and Julius Reuter of London, July 6, 1868. It conveyed the exclusive right to run a cable from Brest, France, to the coast of the United States, and to work it for twenty years, from September 1, 1869, under the following conditions: No soil foreign to France and the United States to be touched by the cable in its transit; the price of a despatch of twenty words not to exceed $20; and the French government binding itself not to grant any other concession for lines between France and North America during the period of twenty years from the first of September, 1869.

The concession having been secured, the new company was organized with good energy. Its capital was fixed at $6,000,000, divided into 60,000 shares of $100 each. In less than eight days the subscription list was filled by the most respectable banking houses in Europe and the shares were immediately sold at the London and Paris Exchanges at a premium of two to three per cent. The first payment of $1,000,000, was made on the day the subscription closed to the Telegraph Construction and Maintenance Company, in England, as an advance upon its disbursements. This company, which had manufactured the former Anglo-American cable, was, by reason of its immense wealth and facilities, the only one ready to undertake the still more difficult and costly contract for the French cable.

7

THE ROUTE.

A survey of routes of the cable was instituted, and has been continued at propitious seasons up to the time of the sailing of the cable fleet. The route ultimately selected — along which the most careful soundings were made under the supervision of expert scientific men and seamen—is from Brest, France, under the Atlantic to the southern edge of the "Grand Bank"; thence to the French island of St. Pierre-off the south coast of Newfoundland; and thence down past Cape Breton Island and Nova Scotia to Boston. The length of cable from Brest to St. Pierre is 2,584 miles; from St. Pierre to Duxbury about 749 miles. The line will then have a length of 3,333 miles from end to end, nearly 1,200 miles more than the length of the Anglo-American cable.

The average depth of the submarine plateau of the French cable is considerably less than that which the present cable between this country and Ireland traverses, and was recommended by Capt. James Anderson, formerly of the Great Eastern.

THE CABLE BED.

The main cable, extending from deep water off Brest to the junction with the shore end at St. Pierre, lies on one of those great plateaus which are known to exist at the bottom of the Atlantic, on one of which the cable between Newfoundland and Valentia has been laid. This plateau, however, is much higher than that occupied by the English cable. By keeping in the five hundred fathom line upon Milne Bank and around the southern edge of the Grand Bank, there is no possibility of ice, or any other agency that can be suggested, injuring the cable. The northern edge of the Grand Bank was avoided, because it is uncertain at what depth the icebergs ground. They are said, upon good authority, to ground at times in ninety fathoms. It is not certain at what depth the vessels employed in the seal trade may choose to drop an anchor sometimes for the purpose of keeping their station in the track of the ice floes. These dangers are avoided in the track chosen for the French cable. Further, the track from the southern edge of the Grand Bank to St. Pierre, and thence to the place of landing at Duxbury, is entirely free from any danger from ice, and does not cross any anchorage resorted to by the fleet of fishing vessels. The cable upon Milne Bank, and from the Grand Bank to St. Pierre, and thence to America (upwards of 1,200 miles), will be laid in water of such easy depth that repairs will be a matter of certainty.

The cable, as now laid, starts in very shallow water from Minou Bay, but in four or five miles it deepens from seventeen to twenty fathoms, and then gradually shelves from thirty to sixty-eight and ninety fathoms. At this level, but on the whole gradually deepening, it continues till in a line with the westernmost part of the Irish coast, where taking a northern course it passes down a gentle slope of sand that continues descending till the depth increases from two hundred to eight hundred and nine hundred fathoms. Over all the rest of the course to mid-ocean the bottom is mud, shells and sand, and with a uniform depth of about two thousand and two thousand two hundred fathoms. At these great depths there is an absolute cessation of all motion. Over such a bottom the line is taken in an arc of a large circle, the most southerly point of the cable being in forty-two degrees north latitude, and the most northerly forty-eight degrees. Along the southern end of the Newfoundland Bank it is sunk in about one hundred and fifty to two hundred fathoms, the water on the Bank itself varying from fifty to ninety fathoms. Thus it is completely sheltered from ice, which, if the icebergs pass the Bank at all, must clear the cable which lies under its lee by some hundred fathoms or more. From this point it is taken up due north in the channel between the Green Bank and the St. Pierre Bank in an almost unvarying depth of five hundred fathoms. From this point out the course is over very regular shoal water, so to speak — being at no part less than one hundred fathoms, and generally over one hundred and fifty — to its termination.

THE NEW CABLE

constructed for the French company is considered decidedly superior to the Anglo-American cable, that is now working across the Atlantic, in that it has greater *conductivity*. The central copper coil, which is the spinal cord — the nerve along which the electric fluid is to run — is larger. It is four instead of three sizes in circumference; that is, it weighs four hundred instead of three hundred pounds the mile. To secure insulation, the wires are imbedded in Chatterton's compound, a preparation impervious to water, and then covered with four successive layers of gutta percha. Outside of these, encasing the whole, is a spiral net of steel wires, each wire surrounded separately with five strands of Russian or Manila hemp, saturated with a preservative compound. The entire cable, while it has the strength of an iron chain, has, at the same time, sufficient elasticity to yield like a rope to the variations of the ocean bed and motion of the waves and currents. It is divided into six sections, viz: the two shore ends, the deep sea section (from off Brest to St. Pierre,) the western and eastern shore ends at that island, and the section laid thence to the Massachusetts coast.

A commission of scientific men, connected with the enterprise, made at the request of Messrs. D'Erlanger and Reuter, a report on the wire, estimating its actual strength at $7\frac{3}{4}$ tons, while the strain required for its immersion could only be 14 cwt. The commission has been sustained in its favorable report by the eminently successful result. It was further stated that the power of transmitting messages through long submarine lines is no longer a matter of doubt, and the laws affecting their transmission are well understood. They promise with certainty that it will be possible to send through the enlarged core twelve words per minute, and by improved methods of signalling it is hoped that this can be exceeded.

THE CABLE FLEET.

The experience of the past had shown that a large vessel was best adapted to the business of consigning to its ocean bed a submarine cable, and as the Great Eastern had once successfully performed a similar mission, and has never been proved to be adapted to anything else, for which reason she has for years been laid up in ordinary, her services were early secured for the duty which she has once more successfully accomplished. The great ship has been perfected in various ways within the past year, a marked improvement being the application of steam power to the government of the rudder, and so perfect is the control attained by this means, that one man standing at his place near the centre of the ship can, with a turn of his hand, control the huge vessel in the heaviest weather.

The big ship took the cable for the first and main part of the line of communication. Material alterations were made in the arrangements of the ship to enable her to carry the large extra weight beyond that of the Anglo-American cable. The main tank was increased to the enormous diameter of 75 feet, and held 1,112 miles of cable. Her after tank contained 912 miles, and the fore-tank 728 miles. The machinery was substantially the same as that used so successfully upon the last occasion. The wheels at the bow and stern, the paying-out and winding-up apparatus, the break machine, the long trough for the cable — all were the same; and near the stern were great red iron buoys for buoying the cable when necessary.

The Great Eastern was accompanied by three consort vessels. Of these the Chiltern proceeded to Brest and laid the heavy shore cable, some six miles in length. The end of this was buoyed until the arrival of the great ship. The Great Eastern, upon her arrival, attached the main rope to this end, and proceeded upon her way to St. Pierre, accompanied by the Chiltern and Scanderia. Each of these vessels carried a portion of the cable, and was furnished with grappling-irons, buoys and picking-up machinery precisely similar to those on board the Great Eastern. The William Cory came on in advance with a portion of the cable, and laid the heavy shore end at St. Pierre, buoying the end in readiness for attachment to the main cable upon the arrival of the Great Eastern. The remaining portion of the cable on board the William Cory was then used, a splice to be effected to the line on board the Scanderia, the length to be completed with the portion borne by the Chiltern, and the line thus be finished to Duxbury.

GETTING AWAY.

On the 11th of June a banquet was had on board the Great Eastern, at which were present Sir Daniel Gooch, M. P., Chairman of the Telegraph Construction and Maintenance Company; Messrs. John Pender, Ralph Elliot, Thomas Brassey, M. P.; Captain Sherard Osborn, Sir Samuel Canning, Mr. Julius Reuter, Sir James Anderson, Mr. Varley, Prof. Jenkin, Baron D'Erlanger, Lord Hay, Lord Houghton, Mr. Elliot, Mr. J. B. Burt, Secretary of the Anglo Mediterranean Company; Mr. R. Slater, Secretary of the French Cable Company; Mr. T. Crampton, the layer of the first successful submarine cable, and many others. The visitors examined the various details of the arrangements for laying the cable, and after having been seated at the table, Sir D. Gooch proposed the toast, " Prosperity to the French Cable Company." This was warmly responded to by Lord Hay, who stated that the Company had the highest reasons to be grateful to the Construction Company for the manner in which they had performed their work. The cable was excellent in its work, and had been completed eighteen days under the stipulated time. Baron D'Erlanger proposed the toast of the day, " Success to the great work of laying down the cable." This was briefly responded to by Mr. Pender and Lord Houghton, and before separating the company expressed their best wishes to Captain Halpin, the commander of the Great Eastern, that the enterprise might be crowned with the success it deserved.

The Great Eastern left the Thames at half-past 11 o'clock on the 12th of June, and proceeded to Brest, and left that port for St. Pierre on the morning of the same month, many bumpers to the success of her voyage having been drank at a banquet in Brest the previous evening.

ST. PIERRE.

When the French government granted permission to lay a cable from Brest it was stipulated that no soil foreign to France and the United States should be touched in its transit, and so St. Pierre, one of the group of small French islands which is supposed to have been known to the Basque fishermen before the Northmen discovered Vinland, lying on the southwest coast of Newfoundland, came to be the first landing place. It is so rocky as to wholly preclude vegetation of the tenderer sort, but has had an interest to the French government because large fishing fleets have for years been sent out there, by the inducement of liberal bounties. These fleets employ as many as twelve thousand men at St. Pierre and the Great and Little Mique-lon Islands, which form the group. The population subsist entirely by fishing. The cod, herring and whale fisheries have proved very pro-ductive, and France has had the sagacity to hold fast by her little North American nursery. It is added, moreover, that for a year past France has been industriously accumulating military stores at St. Pierre, but for what purpose is not definitely known.

TWO HOURS WITH THE FRENCH CABLE.

[From the *Boston Daily Advertiser*, August 31, 1869.]

A small party of scientific gentlemen, members of the American Association for the Advancement of Science, which closed its sessions at Salem last week, received and accepted an invitation on Thursday, 26th instant, to visit the cable office in Duxbury. From Boston to Kingston station by rail thirty-three miles, thence by coach five miles, brought the party to the landing. In an old, but well-preserved, clap-board mansion of that quaint old town were found the headquarters of this new and wonderful highway. The visitors were cordially wel-comed by the manager, Mr. Brown, and were at once brought into the presence of the flitting, flame-like image which indicated, in symbols on a graduated screen, the thoughts working at that instant on the other side of the Atlantic. Interpreting the fitful tremor of the image, or line of light, one inch in length and one-eighth of an inch in breadth, the youthful interpreter, who did not look the wizard that he was,

OLD BANK BUILDING. Terminus of Telegraph at Duxbury.

calmly read, for transcription by his assistant, a message in which occured at intervals the words "New Orleans"—"Citizens"—etc., etc. While inspecting the apparatus the members of the party received the following message fresh from France, sent expressly to them:

"To Duxbury, from Brest—Time 5:20 p. m. [Paris Time.]
"The company present their compliments to the gentlemen assembled at Boston, and hope to be able to send them news of the great international boat race that will be gratifying to both nations."

The usual rate of transmission from Brest to St. Pierre is about ten or twelve words per minute, and from St. Pierre to Duxbury about twenty words. Looking for the mechanism by which these wonderful results were obtained, the inquiring visitors observed on their right placed on a marble pedestal, a medium-sized spool of silk-covered copper wire, said to consist of several thousand turns or convolutions, in the centre of which spool, suspended by a single silk-worm fibre, was a minute mirror attached to a little magnet made from a piece of watch spring. From a lamp properly placed and shaded a beam of light was thrown upon this mirror, and from the mirror was reflected two hundred times enlarged upon the graduated screen in front of the interpreter, the flame-like image already mentioned. In transmitting from Duxbury to Brest, the operator with his right hand makes use of two keys or springs, one of which, being pressed, causes at Brest a deflection in a similar mirror, sending the image-flame to the right, while pressing the other key deflects the mirror at Brest in the opposite direction, sending the image to the left. Its indications are thus interpreted: a jerk or flitting once to the left and then once to the right denotes the letter *a;* a flitting once to the right and then three times to the left denotes the letter *b;* and thus letter by letter the words are spelled.

Passing to an adjoining room, the delicate instruments used for testing the electric conduction of the cable are shown—among which are condensers and batteries, rheostats and shunts, bridges, switches and plugs, and, crowning all, the wonderful astatic galvanometer of Sir William Thompson. But possibly it would weary our readers to tell of ohms and megohms, farads and megafarads, volts and microvolts, and all the terminology of conduction, resistance, electrostatic capacity, and continued electrification. It may, however, gratify them to learn that the insulation of the deep-sea cable, between Brest and St. Pierre, has more than doubled in efficacy during the short month which has elapsed since this cable was first committed to the embraces of Old Ocean—as is evinced by the fact that soon after it was laid, the insulation resistance rose to 2,300 megohms, and has since been gradually increasing until it is now 5,000 megohms per nautical mile. This improvement in the insulation of the deep-sea cable is believed to be mainly due to the coldness or diminished temperature to which it is subjected at great ocean depths.

If one would inquire of a cable electrician — what is a megohm ? he might with propriety be told that it is a million ohms. Should he still further inquire — but what is an ohm ? a suitable reply would be, it is the yardstick of the electrician by which he measures the electric condition of *conductors*, and which may be represented by a round wire of pure copper one-twentieth of an inch in diameter, and 240 feet in length, at the temperature of 60 degrees of the Fahrenheit thermometer ; while a megohm, by which he measures the resistance of *insulators*, is a unit, the length of which is a million times as great.

After being duly initiated into the interesting mysteries of cable working and cable book-keeping, the members of the party partook of a sumptuous repast, given by the gentlemen in charge. During this repast, they were agreeably interested by thrilling accounts of various incidents and hairbreadth escapes during the eventful voyage in laying the cable.

Mr. Brown and Mr. Gaines are gentlemen of long experience in connection with the Malta and Alexandria cables. Mr. Smith, who represents the interests of the telegraph construction and maintenance company, has assisted in laying most of the important cables, from the first one that crossed the channel, to this last great triumph. The number of persons engaged in conducting the affairs of the office, and of the land lines, are about a dozen in all; some of them being on duty at all hours of the day and night — for it must be remembered, that when it is midnight at Duxbury it is daybreak at Brest (France), so that a telegram dated, like the one given above, at five o'clock and twenty minutes, P. M., Paris time, is really sent at twelve o'clock and twenty minutes, P. M., Duxbury or Boston time. It may be deemed worthy of remark that in the transmission of messages of business for the public the time recorded is that of Paris, in business for the service of the cable company, Greenwich time — the same as on the original cable between Ireland and Newfoundland — and in the local business of the Duxbury office, Boston time.

After cordially thanking the courteous and efficient manager and his associates, the gentlemen constituting the party terminated their long to be remembered visit at the Cable-house in Duxbury.

COMPLIMENTARY CORRESPONDENCE.

The following interchanges of civilities passed between the Board of Directors of the Franco-American Cable Company and the Mayor of Boston.

On the evening of the 27th of July, at fifteen minutes past seven o'clock, the Directors sent from Paris the following, which was received at the cable house too late to be read at the banquet:

The Board of Directors of the French-American Cable to His Excellency, the Mayor of Boston:

Please accept our sincerest thanks for the kind welcome extended to our representatives. We are happy you should lend your aid to the establishment of our cable, looking upon it as a great enterprise bringing the two countries in closer and more cordial union. While you drink the toast to the two great and friendly nations, our thoughts will follow and we shall drink to the health of those who have so warmly received our representatives on their hospitable shores.

(Signed) ERLANGER.

Subsequently Mayor Shurtleff received at Boston the following telegram sent from London:

LONDON, July 28, 1869.

The Mayor of Boston:

The Board of the French Atlantic Telegraph Company return their warmest thanks for the splendid reception accorded in the United States to their undertaking.

The good will thus exhibited is sincerely reciprocated by the Board, who confidently look to their cable proving the means of uniting still more closely in friendly feelings the people of the two continents.

The cable will now be opened to the public with the least possible delay compatible with the termination of the European land lines.

(Signed) ROBERT SLATER, JUNIOR, *Sec'y.*

The response of the Mayor of Boston was as follows:

EXECUTIVE DEPARTMENT, CITY HALL, BOSTON, 29 July, 1869.

To the Board of the French Atlantic Telegraphic Company, greeting:

The Mayor of Boston, in behalf of his fellow-citizens, acknowledges the kindly expressed sentiments of reciprocal regard; and, rejoicing in the successful accomplishment of the grand enterprise, which will strengthen the bonds of international friendship and the community of the social, moral and intellectual attributes of human nature, returns to the Telegraphic Company the most cordial sentiments of respect, with the best wishes of the Boston people.

NATHANIEL B. SHURTLEFF, *Mayor.*

To ROBERT SLATER, Jr., *Secretary*, London.

8

www.ingramcontent.com/pod-product-compliance
Lightning Source LLC
Chambersburg PA
CBHW022022080426
42733CB00007B/683